HOW MICROSOFT IS HARNESSING NUCLEAR POWER TO ACCELERATE AI'S FUTURE
The Atomic Brain

How the Power of Atoms is Fueling the Next Generation of Artificial Intelligence Technologies

J. Andy Peters

Table of Contents

Introduction

As artificial intelligence continues to evolve, it's reshaping industries and revolutionizing the way we interact with technology. AI is no longer confined to futuristic dreams or experimental labs; it has become an essential part of our daily lives, from self-driving cars to personalized healthcare and beyond. However, this rapid growth comes with an increasing demand for computational power, requiring massive amounts of energy to fuel the complex algorithms and data processing systems that drive AI. As AI models become more sophisticated and data-heavy, their energy consumption is rising exponentially.

This shift in energy demands presents a new challenge for tech companies like Microsoft, one of the leading pioneers in AI development. Known for pushing the boundaries of technology, Microsoft has been at the forefront of creating AI systems that can analyze, learn, and adapt in ways that were once thought impossible. But with these advancements comes an urgent need for a sustainable solution to power the vast infrastructure that supports AI's growth.

Microsoft has long been recognized for its commitment to innovation, but as AI technology becomes more powerful, it's clear that traditional energy sources may not be enough. The question then arises: how does the world meet AI's enormous energy demands without overloading existing grids or relying on unsustainable fossil fuels? The answer may lie in an unexpected place—**nuclear power**. For Microsoft, the future of AI is not just about algorithms and data; it's about finding new, sustainable ways to power the systems that will shape the future.

Nuclear power, often seen as controversial, is emerging as a potential solution to the growing energy crisis, not just for AI, but for the broader challenge of powering tomorrow's technologies in a sustainable way. With its high energy density and relatively low environmental impact, nuclear energy presents a promising avenue for meeting the power needs of AI while minimizing the environmental footprint. This exploration into nuclear power isn't just about solving AI's energy demands; it could redefine how the world approaches the energy crisis altogether, offering a glimpse into a future where technology and sustainability go hand in hand.

As we look toward the future, the intersection of AI and nuclear energy represents more than just an experiment in powering technology; it holds the key to a new era of innovation. By embracing nuclear power, Microsoft is positioning itself at the vanguard of a revolution that could reshape not only the way we power AI but also the way we think about energy, sustainability, and the technological landscape as a whole. This exploration is not just for the AI industry but is a critical piece in the puzzle of global sustainability, with the potential to impact everything from energy production to environmental policy.

The journey into nuclear-powered AI is more than a technological advancement—it's a step toward a future where AI, energy, and sustainability are tightly woven together, forging a path to a cleaner, more innovative world.

Chapter 1: The Growing Power Demands of AI

As artificial intelligence evolves, so does its demand for computational power. AI systems, especially those designed for tasks like deep learning, machine learning, and real-time analytics, require enormous amounts of data to process and interpret. The scale at which these systems operate means that the hardware supporting them needs to be able to handle vast quantities of information in real time, with precision and efficiency.

Consider the role of AI in **cloud computing** and **data centers**, for example. Every time a person accesses a cloud-based service or app, a complex network of servers processes data in milliseconds to deliver results. These servers, housed in massive data centers, use AI to automate processes, monitor performance, and optimize resource use. But the more AI applications grow, the greater the need for servers capable of handling petabytes of data, performing deep learning calculations, and operating at high speeds.

Similarly, **autonomous vehicles** rely heavily on AI to process the constant flow of information from sensors, cameras, and radar systems. These vehicles must analyze data on their surroundings, make decisions, and adjust to changing conditions in real time. Achieving this level of processing requires highly advanced algorithms running on incredibly powerful hardware. The computations involved in making split-second decisions for driving, navigating, and reacting to the environment demand a level of processing power that far exceeds traditional computing systems.

AI-driven **real-time analytics**—whether in finance, healthcare, or business—also requires immense computational resources. For instance, in healthcare, AI algorithms are used to analyze medical images, predict patient outcomes, and optimize treatment plans, all of which need vast amounts of data and processing power to generate reliable insights. In industries like finance, AI systems analyze market data, spot trends, and make rapid predictions, all in real time, which requires hardware capable of executing complex calculations at lightning speed.

As AI systems grow more sophisticated, their underlying technologies—such as **machine learning** and **neural networks**—become even more computationally intensive. Neural networks, for example, simulate the way the human brain processes information, with thousands of interconnected nodes that require constant recalibration during training. The training of these networks, especially in deep learning, demands immense processing power to adjust weights and biases across millions of parameters.

Advancements like **reinforcement learning** or **transformer models**—used in language processing and other tasks—further escalate the need for high-performance computing. These models often require multiple iterations, running on specialized hardware like **Graphics Processing Units (GPUs)** or **Tensor Processing Units (TPUs)**, which are designed to handle large-scale parallel computations. Without such powerful hardware, scaling these systems or improving their accuracy would be nearly impossible.

As AI moves from theory into real-world applications, the need for computational power is becoming a bottleneck. The systems that currently support AI's capabilities are reaching their limits, and the demand for more efficient, scalable energy sources is becoming ever more pressing. This is where alternative energy solutions, such as nuclear power, come into play. To maintain the momentum of AI innovation while addressing its energy needs, tech companies like Microsoft are exploring new ways to meet these challenges—paving the way for a future where AI can continue to scale without compromise.

As AI technology progresses, the energy required to support it grows at an exponential rate. For companies like Microsoft, this presents a significant challenge. The traditional power sources that have historically fueled data centers and computing infrastructure—such as **coal**, **natural gas**, and even **solar** and **wind**—are often insufficient, unreliable, or unsustainable in the long run.

Coal and **natural gas** have long been the dominant sources of energy for large-scale computing operations due to their reliability and relatively low upfront costs. However, these fossil fuels contribute to environmental degradation and climate change, with carbon emissions that harm both the planet and public health. As the world moves toward cleaner, more sustainable energy solutions, relying on these sources becomes increasingly problematic, especially for companies committed to reducing their carbon footprints.

On the other hand, **renewable energy sources** like **solar** and **wind** offer a cleaner alternative but come with their own set of challenges. While they are environmentally friendly, solar and wind energy are not always dependable. Solar power is only generated during the day, and wind energy fluctuates depending on weather conditions. For AI systems, especially those running 24/7 in high-demand environments like data centers, the intermittency of these renewable sources presents a problem. Energy storage systems, like batteries, are costly and still not capable of meeting the immense, continuous energy requirements of large-scale AI operations.

This brings us to the potential solution that is beginning to capture the attention of Microsoft and other technology giants: **nuclear power**. Unlike solar and wind, nuclear energy is highly efficient, capable of producing large amounts of energy consistently without the fluctuations that renewable sources experience. A single nuclear plant can provide the steady, reliable energy required to power thousands of AI systems simultaneously, without the need for constant adjustments or storage solutions. Moreover, nuclear energy generates minimal carbon emissions, making it an appealing option for companies seeking to balance both high energy demand and sustainability.

For Microsoft, nuclear power offers a pathway to future-proofing their operations. It could not only meet the growing energy demands of their AI systems but also align with their ambitious goal to reach carbon neutrality. With nuclear energy, they could power their AI-driven data centers efficiently and reliably, paving the way for an energy solution that supports the exponential growth of artificial intelligence while ensuring long-term environmental sustainability.

Chapter 2: The Role of Nuclear Power in Technology

Nuclear energy operates through a process called **nuclear fission**, where the nuclei of certain atoms, most commonly **uranium-235** or **plutonium-239**, are split into smaller fragments. This splitting releases an enormous amount of energy in the form of heat. The heat generated from nuclear fission is then used to produce steam, which drives turbines connected to electrical generators. Essentially, nuclear reactors harness this heat to create electricity in much the same way a traditional power plant uses the heat from burning coal or natural gas. The key difference, however, is that nuclear energy uses much less fuel to produce a far larger amount of energy.

One of the most significant advantages of nuclear energy is its **energy density**. Unlike fossil fuels that require large quantities of fuel for relatively small energy outputs, nuclear power can generate vast amounts of electricity with a very small amount of radioactive material. A small pellet of uranium, for example, can produce as much energy as several tons of coal. This makes nuclear power highly efficient, especially for large-scale energy production, and reduces the reliance on vast fuel supplies.

The history of **nuclear energy** stretches back to the mid-20th century, when the discovery of nuclear fission during the 1930s and 1940s opened the door to a new form of energy production. Early nuclear reactors were initially developed for weapons research, but the potential for peaceful energy use quickly became apparent. By the 1950s and 1960s, nuclear power plants were built worldwide, offering a new source of energy that didn't rely on burning fossil fuels. The first commercial nuclear power plant went live in the United States in 1958, and nuclear energy became seen as a promising solution to meet growing global energy demands.

Despite its early promise, the development of nuclear energy has faced several hurdles. High initial costs, concerns over safety—especially following disasters like **Chernobyl** in 1986 and **Fukushima** in 2011—and the long-term issue of **radioactive waste disposal** have slowed its adoption in many countries. These factors, combined with the rise of cheap natural gas and the growing availability of renewable energy sources, have led some to question nuclear energy's place in the future energy mix.

However, in recent years, nuclear energy has been re-examined as a potential solution to the world's energy and environmental challenges. Unlike fossil fuels, nuclear energy does not produce **greenhouse gases** during operation, making it an attractive option for reducing **carbon emissions** and combating climate change. As the world shifts towards more sustainable energy sources, nuclear power has been increasingly viewed as a **clean**, **reliable**, and **scalable** energy solution capable of providing the large amounts of power needed to support future technological advancements, like artificial intelligence.

With the development of newer, safer reactor designs—such as **small modular reactors (SMRs)**—and advances in nuclear waste management, nuclear energy is beginning to regain favor as a potential cornerstone of the clean energy future. In particular, it is being considered as a reliable **baseload energy source** that could complement **renewable energy sources** like solar and wind, which are intermittent and variable.

As countries and companies look for ways to meet the growing demand for energy while reducing their environmental impact, nuclear power is poised to play a pivotal role. For **Microsoft** and other tech giants relying on massive computing power for AI and other advanced technologies, nuclear energy offers an appealing solution to meet their increasing energy needs without the environmental baggage of fossil fuels.

Nuclear power is increasingly viewed as a **promising solution** to meet the rising energy demands of AI, particularly because of its unmatched **efficiency** and **sustainability**. As AI systems grow more complex and require increasingly powerful hardware, the energy needed to run large-scale computing infrastructure also multiplies. Traditional power sources like coal, natural gas, and even renewable energy sources like solar and wind can struggle to provide the consistent, high-density energy needed to power these systems. This is where nuclear energy stands out.

One of the most compelling reasons nuclear energy is considered a viable solution for AI's power needs is its **high energy density**. A small amount of nuclear fuel can produce an enormous amount of energy, which makes it an ideal candidate for industries that require large-scale, continuous power generation. Unlike fossil fuels, nuclear energy does not produce harmful greenhouse gases, making it a much cleaner alternative to traditional power sources. It also has the potential to generate **base-load power**, meaning it can provide a steady, reliable supply of energy 24/7, regardless of weather conditions or time of day—something solar and wind power cannot always guarantee.

In addition to its energy density, nuclear power is well-known for its **long-lasting** fuel, which makes it ideal for applications that require sustained energy without the need for constant re-fueling. The track record of nuclear power in other industries highlights its **proven reliability** and adaptability to high-demand environments.

For example, **nuclear-powered submarines** have been using compact nuclear reactors for decades, allowing them to operate underwater for extended periods without needing to refuel. This same principle applies to **space exploration**, where nuclear power has been used to fuel spacecraft, such as the **Voyager** missions, that have traveled millions of miles from Earth. These industries rely on nuclear energy not just for its energy efficiency, but for its ability to deliver **reliable, high-powered energy** in remote and demanding conditions, much like the energy needs of AI-driven data centers or supercomputing systems.

As AI technology continues to evolve, the need for clean, efficient, and reliable power grows. Nuclear energy offers a unique solution that can keep pace with this demand while also addressing the sustainability concerns that come with relying on traditional fossil fuels. By harnessing the power of atoms, nuclear energy could play a pivotal role in fueling the next generation of AI technologies, all while minimizing environmental impact.

Chapter 3: Microsoft's Vision for AI and Nuclear Energy

Microsoft has made sustainability a cornerstone of its long-term strategy, particularly as it continues to expand and innovate in the field of artificial intelligence. The company understands that the energy demands of AI will only increase as the technology matures, and as such, it has taken bold steps to ensure that its growth doesn't come at the expense of the planet. At the heart of this effort is Microsoft's commitment to achieving **carbon neutrality** across its global operations. This includes not only reducing the carbon emissions from its data centers and office buildings but also rethinking how it powers its vast network of AI systems.

In 2020, Microsoft announced a **historic climate pledge**, setting a goal to become **carbon negative by 2030**. This means that by the end of the decade, the company aims to remove more carbon from the environment than it emits. The company is not only focusing on reducing its direct emissions but also on **eliminating its historical carbon footprint**—a bold move that places Microsoft at the forefront of corporate environmental responsibility.

To meet this ambitious target, Microsoft has been exploring a variety of energy sources that align with its sustainability goals. This includes **renewable energy**, like wind and solar, but the company has also been looking into **nuclear power** as a clean and reliable source of energy that can meet the high demands of AI while ensuring sustainability. By investing in **advanced nuclear technologies**, Microsoft hopes to both power its AI infrastructure efficiently and reduce its reliance on fossil fuels. This forward-thinking approach is part of the company's broader strategy to push the boundaries of AI development without compromising on environmental stewardship.

In its pursuit of sustainable and reliable energy solutions to meet the growing demands of AI,

Microsoft has turned its attention to **nuclear power**, specifically focusing on **Small Modular Reactors (SMRs)**. SMRs are a new generation of nuclear reactors that are designed to be smaller, more cost-effective, and safer than traditional nuclear power plants. These compact reactors offer a potential solution for powering the energy-intensive operations of AI systems, which require substantial, continuous electricity to run massive data centers and advanced machine learning models.

Microsoft has been proactive in researching and forming strategic partnerships to explore how SMRs can meet the energy demands of its **data centers**—the backbone of its AI infrastructure. In collaboration with **X-Energy**, a leading developer of advanced nuclear technology, Microsoft is investigating the potential for **SMRs** to deliver a stable and efficient energy supply. SMRs, by their design, can produce the necessary amount of electricity for large-scale data centers without the need for significant infrastructure expansion or the environmental costs associated with fossil fuels.

These reactors, which are significantly smaller than traditional nuclear reactors, are designed to be safer, scalable, and easier to deploy. Their smaller size means that they can be placed closer to AI data centers, minimizing energy transmission losses and improving efficiency. Additionally, SMRs are designed to be **modular**, meaning they can be scaled up or down depending on the specific needs of the facility, allowing for a more flexible and cost-effective approach to powering AI operations.

Microsoft's **nuclear energy research** also extends beyond just technical exploration. The company is working closely with **regulatory bodies** and other stakeholders to navigate the challenges of implementing nuclear technology at scale, particularly in the context of AI data centers. This includes studying the long-term viability and safety of SMRs, as well as their environmental impact. By focusing on **advanced reactor**

designs that use **liquid fluoride thorium reactors (LFTRs)** and other cutting-edge technologies, Microsoft aims to create a path forward for nuclear power that is both **safe** and **sustainable**, aligning with its broader sustainability goals.

Through these efforts, Microsoft is not just betting on the potential of nuclear energy to power AI but is actively working to shape the future of energy in the technology sector. If successful, SMRs could provide an efficient, low-carbon alternative to fossil fuel-powered data centers, helping to meet the energy demands of AI in a world that increasingly relies on digital infrastructure for everything from machine learning to cloud computing and autonomous systems.

As Microsoft delves deeper into the potential of **Small Modular Reactors (SMRs)** to power its AI infrastructure, the company is also keenly aware of the challenges surrounding public perception, safety, and transparency in nuclear energy. Given the historical concerns about nuclear power—ranging from accidents like **Chernobyl** and **Fukushima** to fears about radioactive waste—Microsoft has made it a priority to address these issues head-on, ensuring that its efforts are not only technologically advanced but also socially responsible.

Safety First: Designing for the Future

The first step in ensuring the safe use of nuclear power is working with companies that specialize in developing **next-generation nuclear technologies**. **Small Modular Reactors (SMRs)** are fundamentally different from traditional nuclear reactors. They are designed with **passive safety features**, meaning that in the event of an emergency, these reactors are built to shut down safely without the need for human intervention or external power sources. This self-regulating safety feature reduces the risk of catastrophic failure and provides greater confidence in their safety.

SMRs also have a **smaller reactor footprint**, which allows them to be deployed in locations that are easier to monitor and control. By using **modern, more secure materials** and more efficient cooling methods, these reactors are built with multiple layers of safety. The designs also incorporate advanced features that can automatically detect and address any operational anomalies before they become critical issues.

Engaging the Public: Building Trust Through Transparency

Transparency is another cornerstone of Microsoft's approach. The company recognizes that for nuclear power to gain public acceptance, people need to feel confident in both the technology and the organizations that are deploying it. To that end, Microsoft is committed to clear communication about its nuclear energy projects. This involves publishing details about its partnerships, research findings, and the steps being taken to ensure safety and sustainability.

One of the ways Microsoft is fostering public trust is through its collaboration with regulators, policymakers, and local communities to educate and provide reassurances about the safety and environmental impacts of nuclear power. The company has worked closely with national and international regulatory bodies to ensure that any nuclear power plants it considers are held to the highest safety standards and undergo thorough evaluations.

Addressing Environmental and Waste Concerns

In addition to safety, nuclear energy's environmental impact—particularly **nuclear waste disposal**—is a major concern. Microsoft has been proactive in exploring solutions to this issue. The company is working alongside experts in nuclear waste management to identify methods for the safe and responsible disposal of spent nuclear fuel. Some advancements in **recycling nuclear fuel** and **long-term storage technologies** are already underway, which aim to minimize the environmental footprint of nuclear power.

Microsoft is also committed to using nuclear power in conjunction with its broader strategy of **carbon-negative operations**, ensuring that nuclear energy contributes to the reduction of greenhouse gas emissions and doesn't exacerbate environmental concerns.

Ethical Responsibility and Long-Term Vision

Finally, Microsoft is fully aware of the ethical implications of using nuclear energy. The company's commitment to **corporate social responsibility** means ensuring that its AI-driven initiatives and energy strategies are aligned with the long-term well-being of both people and the planet. Microsoft is committed to fostering an ethical framework that includes rigorous oversight, adherence to environmental regulations, and continuous dialogue with stakeholders, including communities that may be affected by new nuclear facilities.

By taking these careful, deliberate steps to prioritize safety, engage with the public, and ensure transparency, Microsoft is positioning itself as a leader in not only AI innovation but also in the responsible use of **nuclear energy** for sustainable, long-term growth. These efforts reflect the company's belief that the future of AI—and, by extension, our global energy future—can be powered by clean, safe, and efficient energy sources that benefit both humanity and the environment.

Chapter 4: Small Modular Reactors (SMRs): The Future of Nuclear Energy

Small Modular Reactors (SMRs) are a new generation of nuclear reactors designed to offer several advantages over traditional large-scale nuclear power plants. At their core, SMRs operate on the same principle of nuclear fission, where atoms of uranium or plutonium are split to release energy. However, their smaller size, modular design, and advanced safety features set them apart from conventional reactors.

Unlike traditional nuclear plants, which can be massive, complex, and expensive to build and maintain, SMRs are significantly **smaller in size**—typically capable of producing between 50 to 300 megawatts of electricity, compared to the 1,000 megawatts or more generated by traditional reactors. This makes them more flexible and easier to deploy, especially in remote locations or for smaller energy grids.

The **modular design** of SMRs allows them to be built in factories, then shipped and assembled on-site. This reduces construction costs and time, which can otherwise be a significant hurdle with large nuclear plants. The modular approach also allows for scaling up energy production as needed, by adding additional modules rather than building an entirely new plant. This scalability makes SMRs a more adaptable and cost-effective solution for future energy needs, particularly for industries like AI that require flexible, high-density power sources.

One of the most significant advantages of SMRs is their **safety**. Traditional nuclear power plants rely on complex systems and large reactors, making safety a major concern, particularly in the event of a failure or natural disaster. SMRs, however, are designed with passive safety systems, meaning they require no active intervention to shut down safely. In the event of a malfunction, these reactors can naturally cool down without the need for external power or human action, greatly reducing the risk of catastrophic accidents.

In addition to their safety features, SMRs are also more **environmentally friendly**. Unlike fossil fuels, they produce zero emissions during operation. Their smaller size means that they can be integrated with renewable energy systems, helping to create a more balanced and sustainable energy grid. And because they use fuel more efficiently, SMRs generate less waste compared to traditional reactors, making the disposal and management of nuclear byproducts easier to handle.

Overall, SMRs represent a major shift in nuclear energy, offering a safer, more flexible, and cost-effective alternative to traditional nuclear power plants, with the potential to meet the growing energy demands of modern technologies, like AI, without the environmental and financial challenges of larger reactors.

Small Modular Reactors (SMRs) offer several distinct advantages over traditional large-scale nuclear power plants, making them an appealing option for the future of nuclear energy. One of the most significant benefits is the **lower costs and shorter build times** associated with SMRs. Due to their smaller size and modular design, these reactors can be constructed more quickly and with fewer resources. Traditional nuclear plants require extensive infrastructure, complex permitting processes, and years of construction before they are operational. SMRs, on the other hand, can be built in modules, with each unit constructed in a factory and then assembled on-site. This streamlined approach reduces the overall construction time and capital costs, making nuclear energy more accessible and economically viable.

The **enhanced safety features** of SMRs also set them apart from older nuclear technologies. One of the most compelling aspects of SMRs is their **passive safety systems**, which require no active intervention or external power supply to shut down safely in the event of an emergency. Traditional nuclear plants rely on external cooling systems and human intervention to maintain safe operating conditions, which can be prone to failure in extreme situations. In contrast, SMRs are designed to naturally dissipate heat without the need for pumps or complex mechanisms. This makes them inherently safer and less vulnerable to catastrophic events. Additionally, SMRs can be equipped with **remote monitoring and control** capabilities, allowing operators to track performance and intervene if necessary, even from a distance. This is especially useful in reducing human error and improving overall safety.

The **flexibility of SMRs** is another major advantage. Unlike traditional reactors, which are typically built in large, centralized power plants, SMRs can be deployed in a variety of settings, both urban and rural. Their compact size means they can be located in areas with limited space, such as near population centers, or in remote locations where traditional grid infrastructure is lacking. This flexibility allows for the potential to power everything from industrial facilities to small communities or even isolated military bases. The ability to scale up or down, with multiple SMR units working together in a modular fashion, also makes it easier to match energy supply with demand.

Taken together, these benefits—lower costs, shorter build times, enhanced safety, and flexibility—make SMRs an attractive solution to the challenges of providing reliable, clean energy in an increasingly power-hungry world. Whether serving as a backup power source for a growing AI infrastructure or providing energy to underserved regions, SMRs hold the potential to play a crucial role in the future of nuclear power.

Small Modular Reactors (SMRs) align closely with Microsoft's ambitious vision for the future of artificial intelligence, offering a stable, reliable, and scalable power source to support the growing energy needs of AI-driven technologies. As AI continues to advance, its demands on data centers and computational power will only increase. Microsoft is already working at the cutting edge of machine learning, cloud computing, and real-time analytics, all of which require substantial and continuous energy. Traditional power sources—despite their efforts at being sustainable—often struggle to provide the steady, high-density energy that these systems demand.

SMRs, with their **compact and modular design**, offer a solution that can scale alongside Microsoft's rapid growth in AI development. Unlike traditional nuclear power plants, which are often tied to large, centralized grids, SMRs can be deployed in various settings, including remote areas or smaller, distributed locations that are closer to the data centers. This means that Microsoft could set up energy sources near their AI operations without the need for extensive transmission infrastructure, improving both energy efficiency and operational costs.

Moreover, the **reliability and efficiency** of SMRs make them an ideal partner for energy-intensive applications like AI. Unlike solar and wind, which are intermittent and weather-dependent, nuclear energy provides a constant and uninterrupted supply of power, ensuring that AI systems can run smoothly 24/7. This uninterrupted power supply is critical, especially for **machine learning** algorithms that need massive computational resources for training large models and analyzing vast datasets. With SMRs, Microsoft could ensure that its AI infrastructure has the reliable power it needs to support **cloud computing**, **autonomous systems**, and the millions of processes running simultaneously across its global data centers.

The **scalability** of SMRs is another key advantage. As Microsoft continues to expand its AI capabilities, the company could integrate additional SMRs into its energy portfolio to keep pace with growing demands. This flexibility enables the company to respond rapidly to changes in energy consumption, all while maintaining a low carbon footprint. By choosing nuclear power as a cornerstone of its energy strategy, Microsoft is positioning itself to sustainably meet the **long-term demands of AI** while contributing to a greener, more reliable future for all.

In this way, **SMRs** are not just a way to meet the energy needs of Microsoft's AI systems—they are a forward-thinking, sustainable solution that directly aligns with the company's broader goals of **carbon neutrality**, **environmental responsibility**, and **technological leadership**.

Chapter 5: The Technological Synergy: AI and Nuclear Power

The synergy between artificial intelligence (AI) and nuclear energy creates a dynamic partnership that could redefine the future of both sectors. On one hand, nuclear power offers the massive, consistent energy required to fuel the exponential growth of AI technologies. On the other, AI has the potential to optimize the production, distribution, and management of that energy, ensuring efficiency and sustainability in a way that traditional systems cannot match.

AI's role in **optimizing nuclear energy production** is particularly promising. One of the challenges of nuclear power plants is maintaining a **balanced and consistent energy output** that aligns with real-time demand. Unlike fossil fuel plants, which can ramp up or down quickly based on fluctuations in energy usage, nuclear reactors require careful management to avoid inefficiencies or dangerous overproduction. Here, **machine**

learning algorithms can be used to analyze data from power grids, predict energy needs, and adjust the nuclear reactor's operations accordingly. These AI systems can also monitor reactor conditions, anticipate maintenance needs, and reduce downtime by identifying potential issues before they escalate into problems. For example, AI can predict the wear and tear on reactor components and suggest optimal times for maintenance, minimizing operational disruptions.

Moreover, **AI can aid in the distribution of nuclear energy**, ensuring that the power generated is efficiently allocated to where it is most needed. Through **real-time predictive analytics**, AI systems can assess energy consumption patterns across regions and industries, adjusting the flow of electricity to avoid waste and ensure that data centers—vital for AI processing—receive the power they need without overloading the grid. This real-time adaptability ensures that the energy demands of high-performance computing (HPC) systems, like those used for AI training, machine learning, and deep learning applications, are met without burdening other parts of the grid.

At the same time, nuclear power plants can provide the enormous amounts of **stable and continuous power** required for large-scale AI computations. AI technologies such as **cloud computing**, **machine learning**, and **real-time analytics** demand massive data processing capabilities, which in turn require huge amounts of energy. Traditional energy sources may struggle to meet these demands, but nuclear power—specifically **Small Modular Reactors (SMRs)**—can generate the high-density energy needed without the environmental impact of fossil fuels.

The future of AI and nuclear energy is undoubtedly interwoven. As **AI optimizes the operational efficiency of nuclear plants**, nuclear power in turn becomes the steady backbone of the next generation of AI technologies. This symbiotic relationship allows both fields to evolve together, ensuring that AI-driven systems have the necessary power to achieve breakthroughs in a sustainable, efficient manner. In turn, the ability of AI to manage and monitor energy generation opens up new frontiers for both industries, providing scalable solutions to the world's growing energy and technological needs.

AI's **efficiency in power management** can play a crucial role in maximizing the potential of nuclear energy while ensuring sustainability. By leveraging machine learning algorithms and advanced analytics, AI can help to balance energy supply and demand in real time, ensuring that nuclear power plants operate at optimal levels without overproducing or underproducing energy. This ensures that the immense power generated by nuclear reactors is used most efficiently, minimizing waste and maximizing output. AI-driven **predictive models** can anticipate spikes in energy demand, allowing for dynamic adjustments to energy production, distribution, and storage systems. This optimized approach not only increases the efficiency of nuclear power generation but also contributes to a **sustainable energy ecosystem**, where excess energy can be stored or redirected to other sectors as needed.

For AI systems themselves, nuclear power provides the stable, **high-density energy** needed to run computationally intensive tasks. As AI grows more sophisticated, tasks such as training large neural networks or running complex data models require immense processing power. Traditional power sources may struggle to keep up with these demands, leading to inefficiencies or potential downtimes. Nuclear power, however, offers **consistent and scalable energy**, which is ideal for supporting AI's most demanding operations. **Data centers**, which house the computing infrastructure for AI, can benefit significantly from this reliability, leading to smoother operations, fewer interruptions, and **faster processing speeds**.

Moreover, nuclear-powered AI systems could lead to **quicker training of neural networks**. Training AI models—particularly deep learning models that rely on massive datasets—requires immense computational power. The higher the computational capacity, the faster and more efficiently the model can learn and improve. With the stable and continuous power provided by nuclear energy, AI systems could potentially train models much quicker than they currently do with traditional power sources. The result? More rapid breakthroughs in machine learning and a **reduction in energy consumption** per task, as AI becomes more efficient in how it processes data and makes predictions.

Nuclear power offers a unique advantage here, providing the consistent, large-scale energy needed to drive the next generation of **AI technologies**, while AI's ability to optimize energy production and consumption ensures that nuclear power can be used more effectively and sustainably than ever before. Together, these technologies are poised to create a future where data processing and AI development are faster, greener, and more efficient than ever before.

Chapter 6: Addressing the Challenges: Safety, Public Perception, and Ethics

The integration of nuclear power with AI systems, while promising, certainly brings up important safety concerns. These concerns are amplified by the high-stakes nature of both technologies—nuclear energy with its long history of potential hazards, and AI with its rapidly expanding role in critical systems. As Microsoft explores the use of **Small Modular Reactors (SMRs)** to power its AI infrastructure, addressing safety is paramount, and the company is investing heavily in ensuring both the **safe operation** of nuclear-powered systems and in **mitigating risks** associated with the technology.

Safe Operation of Nuclear-Powered Systems

To ensure the safe operation of nuclear-powered AI systems, Microsoft is focusing on partnering with leading experts and leveraging the most advanced reactor technologies available. **SMRs**—the reactors being considered by Microsoft—are designed with built-in **fail-safes** and **passive safety systems**. These are self-regulating systems that can bring the reactor to a safe shutdown automatically in the event of an emergency. Unlike traditional reactors, SMRs have smaller cores and are designed to be much safer, even in extreme conditions. Many of these reactors do not require active mechanical systems to function, reducing the risk of operator error or system malfunction.

Moreover, **AI-driven monitoring** will play a central role in maintaining safety. Microsoft can use AI systems to monitor reactor performance in real-time, predict potential failures, and immediately implement preventative measures. For example, machine learning algorithms can analyze vast amounts of operational data to detect any anomalies or trends that might indicate a problem, allowing for immediate corrective action to be taken before a serious issue arises.

Safeguards in Place

The safeguards to be implemented in nuclear-powered systems are a combination of **advanced reactor designs, AI-enhanced monitoring**, and **rigorous safety protocols**. For instance:

1. **Real-time AI Monitoring**: AI systems will monitor the reactors and associated infrastructure continuously, analyzing data such as temperature, pressure, radiation levels, and flow rates. AI can also be used to predict and prevent failures based on historical data and predictive models.

2. **Automatic Shutdown Features**: SMRs are designed to shut down automatically in the event of an issue, without the need for human intervention. The **passive safety** design of these reactors means they can cool themselves without external power sources, ensuring that the reactor remains safe even during emergencies.

3. **Remote Operation and Control**: As nuclear-powered AI systems would operate in a highly automated and remote capacity, **remote control and monitoring systems** will be implemented, allowing experts to manage the reactors from afar. This minimizes human exposure to potential hazards and improves response times in case of emergencies.

Mitigating Radioactive Waste Concerns

One of the most persistent concerns with nuclear power has been the issue of **radioactive waste** and its long-term management. Microsoft is aware of this challenge and is working closely with nuclear experts to address it. Modern nuclear technologies, particularly **SMRs**, are designed to be more efficient in terms of fuel use and waste generation. These reactors use **advanced fuel cycles** that produce less nuclear waste and can often reprocess the fuel to be used again, significantly reducing the volume of waste that needs to be stored.

In addition, some of the new SMR designs incorporate **closed-loop systems** that minimize the production of waste by recycling spent fuel within the reactor. These reactors also have the potential to be designed to **run on existing stockpiles of nuclear waste**, offering a novel way of reducing the environmental footprint of traditional nuclear waste storage.

Steps to Mitigate Potential Accidents

While the risks of accidents cannot be entirely eliminated, Microsoft is committed to ensuring that the nuclear-powered systems used for AI are as safe as possible. The company is focusing on **reducing human error**, which is often the cause of incidents in traditional nuclear plants. By incorporating **automated safety protocols** and **AI monitoring**, human intervention will be minimized, and any errors can be identified and corrected immediately.

Further, SMR technology offers **inherent safety** that limits the possibility of catastrophic failure. The reactors are designed to be smaller and operate at lower pressures, meaning they are less likely to experience a meltdown. The use of **natural cooling systems** and **advanced containment technologies** ensures that even if there were to be an emergency, the consequences would be far less severe than in traditional plants.

Public Perception and Transparency

Understanding the concerns surrounding nuclear power, Microsoft is also focused on public **acceptance** and **transparency**. The company recognizes that for nuclear energy to be widely accepted, there must be full transparency about the safety measures in place and a clear commitment to responsible, sustainable practices. This includes working with local governments, regulatory agencies, and environmental groups to ensure that the community's concerns are addressed and that the highest safety standards are met.

Additionally, Microsoft plans to provide **public access to performance data**, offering an unprecedented level of transparency for the operation of these nuclear-powered systems. This will help to build trust and ensure that any potential risks are closely monitored and communicated effectively.

In conclusion, while the integration of nuclear power into AI infrastructure may raise valid safety concerns, Microsoft is making concerted efforts to ensure that these challenges are addressed comprehensively. By leveraging **next-generation reactor technologies**, **AI-driven monitoring systems**, and **advanced safety protocols**, Microsoft is working to ensure that its nuclear-powered systems are not only safe but also **sustainable, efficient**, and **reliable**—driving the next generation of AI innovation without compromising safety or public trust.

The public perception of nuclear energy has long been shaped by past incidents like the **Fukushima**

disaster in 2011 and the **Chernobyl meltdown** in 1986. These high-profile nuclear accidents have instilled deep fear and skepticism about the safety of nuclear energy, leading many to question its viability as a clean and reliable energy source. In this context, **Microsoft** faces an important challenge as it explores the potential of **nuclear-powered AI systems**—to not only secure the trust of the public but to actively **rebuild confidence** in the role of nuclear energy in powering the future of AI.

Building Trust and Ensuring Transparency

To address these concerns, Microsoft recognizes the importance of **transparency** in its efforts to integrate nuclear power with AI technologies. The company is committed to sharing comprehensive information about the **safety measures** it is implementing and the **progress** of its nuclear energy initiatives. This includes public reports on the development and operation of **Small Modular Reactors (SMRs)**, which are often viewed as a safer and more sustainable alternative to traditional large-scale reactors. SMRs have been designed with **advanced safety features**, such as **passive cooling systems** that can automatically shut down the reactor in case of a malfunction, making them less prone to the kind of catastrophic failures seen in older nuclear plants.

Microsoft also aims to work closely with **regulatory bodies** and **nuclear experts** to ensure that it adheres to the highest safety and operational standards. By collaborating with governments, independent scientists, and third-party safety experts, the company seeks to demonstrate its commitment to responsible use of nuclear power and AI. Furthermore, **public engagement** and education will be key. Microsoft plans to invest in **public outreach** efforts aimed at informing people about the safety advancements of modern nuclear technology, as well as the potential benefits of AI-powered energy systems. This effort includes educational campaigns to address misconceptions about nuclear energy, provide clarity about AI's role in improving safety and efficiency, and outline how SMRs are designed to be more secure than their predecessors.

Ethical Dimensions of AI and Nuclear Energy

As the world embraces the combined potential of AI and nuclear power, **ethical considerations** come to the forefront. One of the primary concerns is the **potential misuse of AI-powered nuclear systems**. If AI systems responsible for managing nuclear reactors were to be manipulated or fail, the consequences could be disastrous. Microsoft must ensure that its AI technologies are designed with strict safeguards and are transparent and accountable at every level of operation. This involves developing AI that operates within **clearly defined ethical boundaries** and ensuring that decision-making processes are explainable and auditable. AI's ability to learn and adapt must be tightly regulated, particularly when it comes to critical infrastructure like nuclear reactors, to prevent unintended consequences or malicious exploitation.

Another key ethical concern is the **societal impact** of deploying nuclear energy at scale. While nuclear power has the potential to provide clean, sustainable energy, it also comes with the challenge of managing **radioactive waste** and ensuring long-term safety. The public is naturally wary of these risks, especially given the environmental and health consequences of past nuclear disasters. Microsoft's approach to nuclear energy will need to address these concerns head-on by implementing the most rigorous **waste management protocols** and ensuring that the technology is developed with the future of the planet in mind.

Responsible Use of AI-Powered Nuclear Systems

Microsoft is committed to the responsible use of **AI-powered nuclear systems** by implementing strict oversight and operational transparency. This includes ensuring that **AI systems** are used only for their intended purposes and are **not misused** for harmful activities. The company will need to work with governments, international organizations, and independent auditors to create clear and enforceable guidelines about the use of AI in nuclear energy. By establishing a set of **ethical principles** and **governance frameworks**, Microsoft can ensure that AI is used to enhance safety, improve efficiency, and minimize risks.

Moreover, Microsoft recognizes that **continuous monitoring** and **human oversight** will remain critical components of any nuclear-powered AI system. While AI can optimize and enhance many aspects of nuclear energy production, human decision-makers will still play an essential role in ensuring that these systems function safely and ethically. AI systems will be designed to work **alongside humans**, providing valuable data and insights, but leaving critical decisions in the hands of skilled operators and decision-makers who are guided by clear ethical standards and accountability mechanisms.

In the end, Microsoft's approach to combining AI with nuclear energy will require balancing the immense potential of these technologies with the **responsibility** of ensuring their **safe, ethical, and transparent deployment**. The company must navigate these challenges carefully to ensure that its efforts not only advance the future of AI and energy but also respect public concerns, protect the environment, and benefit society as a whole.

Chapter 7: The Impact on Global Sustainability and the Future of AI

The potential of nuclear-powered AI systems to reshape the global energy landscape is nothing short of transformative. As Microsoft's venture into Small Modular Reactors (SMRs) progresses, it becomes clear that the implications go far beyond simply meeting the immediate energy needs of AI. In a world where energy demands are set to soar, particularly with the increasing reliance on data-intensive technologies, the combination of nuclear energy and AI could provide the stable, scalable power necessary to sustain the technological revolution that is underway.

One of the most significant aspects of this innovation is its **sustainability**. Traditional energy sources, whether fossil fuels or even renewables like solar and wind, face limitations in terms of consistency and scale. Nuclear energy, on the other hand, offers a reliable and efficient solution that can meet the round-the-clock energy demands of AI-driven operations, making it a game changer for industries that rely on massive data processing capabilities. This stability could also pave the way for a **greener future**, where AI is not constrained by energy limitations or environmental impacts, helping to reduce the carbon footprint of digital technologies.

In the long term, this fusion of AI and nuclear energy could drive advancements in fields that are poised to tackle some of humanity's most pressing challenges. Take **climate change modeling**, for example. AI already plays a crucial role in predicting climate patterns, analyzing vast amounts of data to forecast environmental shifts. With access to more reliable and abundant energy, AI could run more complex simulations, process data faster, and develop more accurate models, ultimately contributing to better decision-making in addressing climate crises.

Moreover, in the realm of **personalized healthcare**, AI's ability to analyze genetic data, medical records, and treatment outcomes could be amplified by the increased computational power that nuclear energy enables. With faster and more efficient processing, AI could tailor treatments to individuals with greater precision, leading to better health outcomes and reducing the burden on healthcare systems. This kind of progress could not only enhance patient care but also contribute to the development of new treatments, especially in fields like **drug discovery** or **genomic medicine**, where AI is already making significant strides.

As these technologies advance, the ability to process vast quantities of data without interruption or excessive energy costs will become crucial. The role of nuclear-powered AI in these developments cannot be overstated—it will drive the future of everything from **autonomous vehicles** to **smart cities**, from **sustainable farming** practices to **advanced robotics**. All of these sectors, which rely heavily on AI, stand to benefit from a more stable and powerful energy infrastructure.

Ultimately, the partnership between AI and nuclear energy offers a vision of a future where technology is not only more advanced but also more sustainable. It presents the possibility of a world where the energy needed to power the innovations of tomorrow is abundant, clean, and reliable. The implications for **global energy systems** are profound, and Microsoft's efforts to marry these two technologies could mark a turning point in both the AI and energy sectors, ushering in a new era of innovation that is not only smarter but also more environmentally responsible.

The environmental benefits of nuclear-powered AI systems are substantial, particularly in the context of **reducing carbon emissions** and mitigating our reliance on fossil fuels. As the world grapples with the effects of **climate change** and the urgent need to transition to cleaner energy sources, nuclear power presents a viable, low-carbon alternative to traditional energy sources. Unlike coal, natural gas, and even some renewable energy sources, **nuclear power** produces vast amounts of energy without the harmful carbon dioxide emissions that contribute to global warming.

For tech giants like **Microsoft**, adopting nuclear energy for their AI systems represents a major step toward achieving their sustainability goals. By shifting away from carbon-intensive energy sources and toward **Small Modular Reactors (SMRs)**, Microsoft and other companies can dramatically reduce their carbon footprint while meeting the massive energy demands of AI and machine learning technologies. This shift not only supports Microsoft's ambitious **carbon neutrality targets** but also sets a powerful example for the entire tech industry.

The adoption of nuclear energy in powering AI systems could spark a **wider trend** across the tech sector. As AI continues to advance and becomes more integrated into industries ranging from healthcare to finance, the energy demands will only grow. The environmental impact of running massive AI data centers could soon become a critical factor in how companies approach their energy needs. In this light, nuclear power, particularly the innovative and **safe technologies like SMRs**, offers a **scalable solution** to sustain the industry's future growth while maintaining environmental responsibility.

Other tech companies, from Google to Amazon, could follow Microsoft's lead in exploring **nuclear energy** as a cleaner, more efficient way to power their expanding AI infrastructures. As these companies face mounting pressure to **reduce carbon emissions** and operate more sustainably, nuclear energy could become a critical part of their energy mix, making the entire industry more resilient to energy crises and accelerating the transition to a **greener tech ecosystem**. The combined power of AI and nuclear energy could ultimately create a **synergistic solution**, where tech companies not only advance in their capabilities but also play a key role in combating

climate change, leading the charge toward a **sustainable, carbon-neutral future**.

Chapter 8: What's Next? The Future of AI and Nuclear-Powered Technologies

The fusion of **AI** and **nuclear energy** holds the promise to radically accelerate innovation across several industries. As AI continues to evolve and nuclear power becomes more adaptable, these two technologies could unlock new possibilities, from **space exploration** to **autonomous systems** and **smart cities**. The convergence of AI's computational power with nuclear energy's stable, high-output capabilities offers an ideal foundation for pushing technological boundaries.

In the realm of **space exploration**, the demand for energy-efficient and long-lasting power sources is critical. Nuclear energy, with its ability to generate vast amounts of energy from small amounts of fuel, has already proven its potential in powering spacecraft and rovers, like NASA's **Curiosity Rover** on Mars, which is powered by a **radioisotope thermoelectric generator (RTG)**. Integrating AI with nuclear power could further enhance this by enabling real-time data processing, predictive maintenance, and more efficient energy management for extended missions. AI could autonomously adjust power distribution, optimize energy use, and predict potential failures, ensuring that space missions run smoothly for years without the need for human intervention.

In the case of **autonomous systems**, nuclear-powered AI could enable long-duration, self-sustaining operations, especially for applications like self-driving vehicles or autonomous drones. These systems, which currently rely on conventional battery power, could benefit from a nuclear energy source, providing the sustained, powerful energy needed to operate without frequent recharging. AI could manage the power usage in real time, adjusting energy distribution based on the demands of the vehicle's navigation, data processing, or environmental sensors.

One of the most exciting prospects lies in the development of **smart cities**, where AI and nuclear energy could work in tandem to create intelligent, self-regulating urban environments. These cities could be powered by nuclear energy, with AI managing everything from traffic systems to energy usage, waste management, and public services. By integrating AI with nuclear power, cities could minimize energy consumption, maximize efficiency, and significantly reduce their carbon footprint.

Additionally, one of the most impactful breakthroughs that could arise from the fusion of these technologies is the creation of **fully autonomous energy grids**. These grids could be powered by a mix of **nuclear energy** and managed by **AI systems** that optimize energy distribution in real time. AI could analyze consumption patterns, adjust output from nuclear reactors, and dynamically switch between various energy sources to ensure that the grid is always operating at peak efficiency. These grids would not only be capable of managing energy distribution with minimal human oversight but could also intelligently predict and respond to power demands, effectively reducing waste and enhancing energy security.

Another potential breakthrough lies in the development of **new AI algorithms** designed to **optimize nuclear reactors for maximum energy efficiency**. AI could be used to analyze vast amounts of data from reactors, identifying trends, inefficiencies, and opportunities for improvement that would be impossible for humans to detect. This could include adjusting the reactor's fuel mix, managing waste more effectively, or ensuring more consistent reactor performance. Over time, AI could lead to smarter, more resilient nuclear power plants that are capable of providing even greater levels of clean, reliable energy with less environmental impact.

The fusion of AI and nuclear energy opens up a realm of possibilities across industries. From **space exploration** to **autonomous systems** and **smart cities**, the potential is enormous. By integrating AI with nuclear power, we are not only stepping closer to achieving a more sustainable future but also creating the technological foundation for innovations that could change the world as we know it.

The potential for **AI and nuclear energy** to revolutionize not just tech industries but entire global sectors could pave the way for **widespread adoption of nuclear power** in areas far beyond traditional electricity generation. As the world faces the urgent need to decarbonize and meet energy demands, the combination of AI's precision and nuclear power's ability to deliver massive, clean energy could unlock new possibilities in **transportation**, **agriculture**, and other key industries.

In **transportation**, for instance, nuclear-powered AI systems could lead to the development of highly efficient, clean energy solutions for electric vehicles, ships, or even planes. As AI algorithms become more sophisticated, they could optimize fuel usage, battery life, and energy distribution, making nuclear-powered transportation both viable and sustainable. Autonomous vehicles, already powered by AI, could rely on energy from nuclear reactors designed specifically for mobile or regional energy supply, reducing their dependence on fossil fuels and significantly lowering emissions.

In **agriculture**, nuclear energy could offer an ideal solution for powering large-scale, AI-driven operations, particularly in **food production** and **sustainable farming**. AI algorithms could optimize water use, soil conditions, and crop growth cycles, all while benefiting from the consistent, carbon-free energy provided by nuclear power. This could help meet the growing demand for food globally while reducing the carbon footprint of farming.

The global implications extend even further. As nations grapple with the twin challenges of energy security and climate change, **AI and nuclear energy** could become a cornerstone of new, more sustainable industrial practices. Countries that are rich in natural resources and have stable political climates might lead the charge, but with the right advancements in **SMR technology** and international collaboration, nuclear power could become an attractive solution for both developed and developing nations alike. This, in turn, could accelerate the shift towards a more **decarbonized, energy-efficient** global economy.

In sum, the integration of AI with nuclear energy is not just a game-changer for the tech sector but could spark a much broader **global energy transformation**, creating new, sustainable pathways for industries across the board. The promise of clean, efficient energy—powered by

AI—could soon become a universal standard, touching everything from transportation and agriculture to manufacturing, smart cities, and beyond. The future of global energy may be closer to a **fusion of AI and nuclear power** than ever imagined.

Conclusion

As we stand at the threshold of a new era, the convergence of **artificial intelligence**, **nuclear energy**, and **sustainability** is poised to redefine the way we power the technologies of tomorrow. Microsoft's groundbreaking pursuit of nuclear-powered AI systems is far more than a bold technological innovation; it represents a commitment to shaping a future where energy demands are met with clean, reliable, and scalable power sources. By exploring the fusion of these two transformative forces, Microsoft is laying the groundwork for a future that is not only more efficient but also more sustainable, ushering in a new chapter in the global effort to combat climate change.

This integration of nuclear energy and AI is the beginning of a **paradigm shift** in how we approach energy consumption and technology. By providing the immense power needed to drive AI's exponential growth, nuclear energy becomes a vital enabler of progress. But beyond powering machines, this collaboration between AI and nuclear energy holds the promise of solving some of the world's most pressing challenges. From improving global health through AI-driven diagnostics to accelerating our understanding of climate change through advanced modeling, the possibilities are vast. And as we look to the future, the combination of these technologies could offer the keys to achieving a truly **sustainable** and **resilient world**.

As the journey unfolds, it's clear that the fusion of AI and nuclear energy is not just a technological trend but a necessary evolution—a step towards a more harmonious, energy-efficient, and intelligent world. This could very well be the solution to meeting the world's increasing demands for energy, while reducing our carbon footprint and creating a cleaner, brighter future for generations to come.